TOMORROW'S EARTH

A SQUEAKY-GREEN GUIDE

DAVID BELLAMY

Illustrated by Benoît Jacques

COURAGE
BOOKS

Editor: Heather Amery
Designer: Rowena Alsey
Typesetter: Kerri Hinchon
Production: Sarah Schuman
Cover Design: Toby Schmidt

Edited and designed by
Mitchell Beazley Publishers
Michelin House
81 Fulham Road
London SW3 6RB

Canadian representatives: General Publishing Co., Ltd.,
30 Lesmill Road, Don Mills, Ontario M3B 2T6.
International representatives: Worldwide Media Services, Inc.,
115 East Twenty-third Street, New York, New York 10010.

9 8 7 6 5 4 3 2 1
Digit on the right indicates the number of this printing.
LC# 91-58652
ISBN 1-56138-124-1

Typeset in Quorum ITC
Reproduction by Mandarin Offset, Hong Kong
Printed and bound in Hong Kong by South Sea International Press

Published by Courage Books, an imprint of
Running Press Book Publishers
125 South Twenty-second Street
Philadelphia, Pennsylvania 19103

Contents

Spaceship Earth

Have you ever dreamed of traveling through Space in a spaceship which has everything you, your family and all your friends need? Well, we all live on a type of spaceship. It is a rocky platform, we call Earth, which speeds through space around a star we call the Sun.

Our Spaceship Earth was launched 4,600 million years ago in a giant explosion, called the Big Bang. This explosion created all the stars, planets and everything in the Universe.

Building Blocks

Everything on Spaceship Earth is made of 92 different sorts of atoms, called elements. These are the building blocks which, in different amounts, make up all the plants, animals, rocks, water and the air.

Spaceship Calendar

Four billion years ago, the crust of the Earth was formed. Its rocks were made up of most of the elements, some of which are very common, some very rare.

The atmosphere was full of gases, such as carbon dioxide, methane and ammonia, which would poison us. But these gases contained all the main elements which make up living things.

The gases – hydrogen, carbon dioxide, oxygen and nitrogen – slowly but surely began to form new sorts of chemicals. They were sugars, fats and proteins – the things we need to eat each day to stay alive and healthy.

3½ billion years ago, very simple forms of life grew on the surface of Spaceship Earth. They used the new chemicals to grow.

2½ billion years ago, very simple plant-like forms of life were using the energy of the Sun (solar power) and putting the first oxygen into the sea and the atmosphere.

1½ billion years ago, more complicated life forms were living in the sea. Some were forms of plant life and used the energy of the Sun to grow and make their food. Others were early forms of animal life that ate the plants and each other. They were the ancestors of all the plants and animals alive today, including you and me.

Gradually, these more complicated forms of life took control and began to develop into all the different plants and animals on Spaceship Earth. These are the life support systems on which all life depends.

Spaceship Earth's Clock

Imagine all those billions of years squashed into a 24-hour clock. Spaceship Earth is an amazing place. People like us have only been on board for the last second of that clock. In that time, we have already destroyed more than a third of all the homes of the plant and animal life – the life support systems – and have altered the balance of the rest.

There is a lot of cleaning-up work to be done over the next few years.

Welcome aboard our Spaceship!

Walking Through More Recent Times

1 billion years ago, no animal had walked on Earth.

1 billion months ago, no dinosaur had walked on Earth.

1 billion weeks ago, giant penguins walked on Earth.

1 billion days ago, no two-legged mammals had walked on Earth.

1 billion hours ago, no human being had walked on Earth.

1 billion seconds ago, you hadn't walked on Earth, although your Mom and Dad may have.

How do we know all this? Well, it is all thanks to the fossils – the prints left in rocks by plants and animals which died millions of years ago.

Scientists have found bones, teeth and shells, and even insects' wings, feathers, eggs and footprints. This is Spaceship Earth's flight recorder.

Spaceship Earth and Us

All the people in the world, including you, are the human crew of Spaceship Earth.

We get our water from the rain, air to breathe from the atmosphere, and our food mainly from plants. Spaceship Earth keeps us at the right temperature and protects us from harmful radiation from outer space.

Life Support Systems

The air, water, and all the plants and animals on Spaceship Earth keep you supplied with all the chemicals you need – not too little and not too much. These are the life support systems.

We get our water from the rain, thanks to the sea. We get the oxygen we need to breathe from the atmosphere, thanks to the plants which produce it. We get all the chemicals and other things from our food, thanks again mainly to plants. Our food is also an instant supply of energy to keep us going, growing and in repair. It also keeps us warm.

Your Simple Chemicals

What are people made of ? Take a look in the mirror at wonderful, brilliant you. You are made up of a lot of water and small amounts of some simple chemicals, plus minute traces of a few others.

Water is fantastic stuff. It must be because about 73% of you is water.

Solar Power

The Sun is our nearest star and, like all stars, it is a giant atomic power station. It pours out vast amounts of solar power – sound, heat, light, ultra-violet rays and atomic radiation – into space.

It is mega noisy and mega dangerous, so it is a good thing that it is 93,750,000 miles (150 million km) away. But without the Sun, there would be no sunlight and no life on Earth.

Every year, Spaceship Earth receives 600,000 mega units of energy from the Sun. Each mega unit is enough to boil a kettle of water a day for everybody on the Earth. About 400,000 mega units are used to keep the atmosphere and the sea warm. About 190,000 mega units evaporate water from the surface of the sea and the land to make the rain.

Wind System

Because warm air is lighter than cold air, it rises. As the warm light air rises upward, cold heavier air flows in underneath. The cold air is warmed up and begins to rise, keeping it all on the move. This movement of air makes the winds, and even the hurricanes blow. Wind is moving air. Waves are moving water, powered by about 1,000 of the mega units of energy.

The Tides

As the Moon goes around the Earth, it pulls the seawater up into a bulge, or tidal wave. The wave travels across the oceans, directly underneath the Moon. This causes the tides along the coasts – two high tides and two low tides every day.

Once every two weeks, the Sun and the Moon are in a line and act together, pulling at the water and causing extra high tides. These are called spring tides. Once every two weeks, the pull of the Sun and Moon are not in line. Then we get extra low tides. These are called neap tides.

Fantastic Facts

The greatest tidal rise and fall in the world is in the Bay of Fundy on the southeast coast of Canada – an amazing 45 feet (13.7 meters). Small seas, such as the Mediterranean, only have small tides. There the beaches are not washed by the sea and this is one reason why they get so dirty.

Life Preserving Atmosphere

Around Spaceship Earth there is a blanket of air, 12½ miles (20 km.) thick, called the atmosphere. It protects us from the harmful rays of the Sun but it lets in the light and warmth that all the plants and animals, including us, need to live and to grow.

The atmosphere keeps in the warmth from the Sun. Without it, the whole world would be covered with ice. It provides us with some very important and useful things and protects us from falling space junk and pieces of rock which come from outer space.

Useful Gases

The atmosphere is made up of four gases – nitrogen, oxygen, water vapor and carbon dioxide. It also has dust and many other things in it. The atmosphere is held in position by the Earth's gravity. This is the invisible force that pulls everything toward the Earth. It is the same force that holds us on the Earth.

The Earth's Greenhouse

Nitrogen and oxygen are transparent gases which let all the Sun's rays reach the surface of the Earth. Water vapor is transparent too, until it forms into clouds. These act as sunshades during the day and keep in the warmth from the Sun during the night.

Carbon dioxide is a very special gas because it lets in the heat of the Sun to warm the Earth but does not let it all back out again. It is called a "greenhouse gas," because it acts just like the glass of a greenhouse, trapping the Sun's heat during the day and keeping us warm. Another natural greenhouse gas is called methane.

There is not much carbon dioxide in the atmosphere which is a good thing. If the amount of greenhouse gases increases too much, the Earth could become too hot. If there were not enough, the Earth would cool down. It is all a matter of balance.

Fiery Oxygen

Oxygen is another gas that must be kept in balance. When anything burns, it uses oxygen. Nothing can burn without it. But if there were too much oxygen in the atmosphere, everything would burst into flames, even on a wet day.

Oxygen is a light gas and rises high into the atmosphere. There it absorbs ultraviolet light which turns it into ozone (Sun-burnt oxygen). This is heavier than oxygen and hangs about, forming the ozone layer – a sun screen which blocks the Sun's rays and protects us from sunburn and skin cancer.

At the North and South poles, where the Sun does not shine for six months of the year, less ozone is formed. Here the Sun's rays are not so well blocked and you can get both a sunburned face and frostbite in your toes at the same time.

Shooting Stars

Lumps of rock coming toward the Earth from space are slowed down as they enter the atmosphere. They get hot because they rub against the air – just like the brakes on a bicycle rubbing against the wheel. Because there is oxygen in the atmosphere, they catch fire and burn up before they hit the Earth. This is what shooting stars are.

Useful Nitrogen

Nitrogen is the most plentiful gas in the atmosphere. Every time we breathe in, we take large amounts into our lungs. But our bodies cannot absorb it, so we breathe it out again. If we did absorb it, we would soon die, so it is a good thing that it stays in the air.

The Earth is kept supplied with all the nitrogen we need by tiny water plants, called blue-green algae and bacteria. Some of the bacteria live in special nodules on the roots of plants, such as peas and beans. They take in nitrogen from the atmosphere and make it into a fertiliser in the soil.

Wonderful Water

Water is very special stuff. It is made of two gases – hydrogen and oxygen. There are three forms of water on Spaceship Earth – solid ice, liquid water and water vapor, which is a gas.

The simple chemicals which make up water hang on very tightly to each other. That is why insects, called pond skaters, can walk on water, and why a belly flop into a swimming pool hurts so much.

When liquid water turns into water vapor gas, it uses lots of energy, in the form of heat. When our sweat dries up, or evaporates, it turns into invisible water vapor. It uses the heat from our bodies, so we cool down.

When water is cold enough, it changes from a liquid into solid ice. As it changes, ice crystals form and the freezing water expands, or gets bigger. Ice floats because it is lighter than water. If ice was heavier than water, it would sink to the bottom of the sea and would stay there. The oceans would freeze from the bottom upward.

9

The Life-giving Sea

Salt-water covers nearly three-quarters of the surface of Spaceship Earth. The oceans are home to a great variety of plants and animals, including the highly intelligent whales, dolphins and porpoises. (I bet they call it Spaceship Water!)

The oceans and seas of the world contain 97% of the world's water, an incredible 343 quintillion gallons.

Into the Sea

Every day about 67 trillion gallons of water falls on land. It wears away rocks and dissolves the minerals in them, and carries them down to the sea.

Everything that dissolves in water is, eventually, washed down into the sea. The oceans contain $7^1/_2$ million tons of gold, dissolved in the water.

Cooling the Earth

Lick yourself on a hot day and you will find it tastes salty. When sweat evaporates – or dries – from your skin, it cools you down. It also leaves the salt behind and the sweat becomes pure water vapor.

Every day, 302 trillion gallons of water evaporate from the surface of Spaceship Earth. Leaving the salt behind, it becomes pure water vapor, which forms clouds and eventually falls as rain.

As the water evaporates, it cools the surface of Spaceship Earth. This helps to move the atmosphere about, stirring clouds, causing storms and pure water to fall as rain, hail and snow.

Life in the Sea

Deep down in the sea there is no sunlight at all. On the surface, there is enough to allow tiny floating plants, called plankton, and seaweeds to grow. They trap the energy of the Sun and store it away as sugar and other good-to-eat chemicals.

To do this, plankton take in carbon dioxide dissolved in the sea water and they bubble oxygen out into the sea water and into the atmosphere.

To use the stored energy to grow and swim about, all the plants and animals, including the giant whales and sharks, use up the oxygen in the water and produce carbon dioxide.

Over time, the energy taken in by the plankton and energy used up by the plants and animals should balance the amount of carbon dioxide and oxygen in the sea and in the atmosphere. But it does not always happen like that.

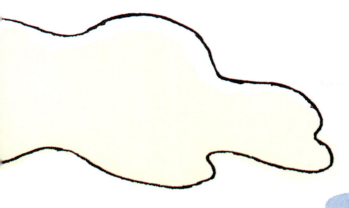

The Little Round Rock Makers
Seawater contains 65 times more carbon dioxide than the atmosphere. It is home to the coccolithophores – a name which means "little round rock makers." These are tiny plants which have tough skeletons made of calcuim and carbon dioxide.

Fossil Fuels
We know that, in the past, all the energy stored by the plants was not used up by the animals. It fell to the bottom of the sea where it formed oil and natural gas. This is some of the energy we now use in our homes and cars.

When they die, their skeletons fall to the bottom of the sea. In time, a long time, they pile up to form sediments which eventually make chalk and limestone rock.

That is how the White Cliffs of Dover, on the south coast of England, and many of the world's great mountains were made, under the water.

Called fossil fuels, they are fossil solar power and fossil carbon dioxide which have been stored out of harm's way for millions of years.

Because the carbon dioxide is locked away in the fossil fuels and the rocks, extra oxygen is released and some bubbles up into the atmosphere. That is why there is so much oxygen and that is probably how it got into the atmosphere in the first place.

About $2\frac{1}{2}$ million years ago, there was no oxygen in the sea or in the atmosphere of Spaceship Earth. The sea was full of iron, dissolved in the water. As soon as there was oxygen, the iron rusted and fell to the bottom of the seas.

Corals, the Reef Rock Makers

If you like swimming, you would love clear sea water which never gets colder than 60°F (15°C), for then you could swim all the year around.

You wouldn't be alone, for the coral animals love clean, warm water, too. As they grow, they help to build and repair enormous walls of rock, called coral reefs, below the low tide mark. These reefs protect the coasts from being worn away by the sea. They are home to thousands of different sorts of plants and animals – snails, worms, crabs, sea stars, fish, turtles and whales.

The Corals

Corals need sunlight to be able to grow well. It is used by tiny plants living in their bodies. The plants make sugar and oxygen which help the corals to make their limestone skeletons with calcium and carbon dioxide from the seawater.

Living coral reefs lock up carbon dioxide and make extra oxygen. This helps to keep the important gases in balance in the sea and in the atmosphere.

Every plant and animal that lives and grows on a coral reef has an important job to do. They help to keep the carbon dioxide and oxygen balance right. They provide homes and food for millions of fish and keep the sea defenses in working order.

The reefs are so strong that they can withstand the strongest waves for many years. Ancient reefs, millions of years old, have been pushed up from under the sea, by forces inside the Earth, and now form parts of large mountains on dry land.

The whole reef is also held together by seaweeds, sponges and fan corals, each playing their part.

Corals grow only in the clear, pure seawater around the Equator. If the water gets too hot, too cold or too dirty, then they soon die and the reefs start to break down and wear away.

If a reef dies and breaks up, it releases carbon dioxide into the atmosphere. It also opens up the coasts to erosion by the sea. Remember, carbon dioxide is a greenhouse gas. If more carbon dioxide ends up in the atmosphere, Spaceship Earth could overheat.

The Deep Blue Sea

Seawater filters the sunlight as it shines through the water. Light is made up of all colors of the rainbow. The sea filters out the colors, starting with the red. The red rays do not get very far, the blue light rays travel the farthest. The deeper you go down, the darker it is and the bluer the water looks.

Below 6,600 feet (2,000 m.), there is no sunlight at all, even in the clearest water. Everything below that lives on food falling from the surface of the sea.

How Coral Reefs Grow

The tiny sea animals that build the reefs are related to jellyfish and sea anemones. They eat minute animals, called plankton, which grow in huge quantities in the sea.

A young coral animal puts out limestone from its body, making a tiny cup of rock which it lives in all its life. Tentacles around its mouth collect the plankton.

When it is big enough, a coral animal grows by sending out branch-like buds. In each bud is another tiny animal with its own skeleton. The process goes on and on, forming massive reefs.

There are two main forms of budding. One, inside the ring of the animal's tentacles, produces the long curving patterns of the brain corals. The other, budding outside the ring of tentacles, produces other patterns.

How Mountains are Made

When coral reefs grow in the sea, the enormous weight of new rock presses down on the edges of the Earth's continents.

Although the continents are huge, we know that they are made of separate rocky plates. The plates float on molten rock under the crust of the Earth. Some people believe that the weight of the coral reefs may push the plates along, moving the continents apart. To fill the gap between the plates, volcanoes erupt on the floor of the oceans. The boiling hot lava, or molten rock, from them gushes out on to the sea floor.

Other people believe that the lava pushes the plates apart. Perhaps it is a bit of both. One day we will know. Perhaps you will be one of the scientists who helps to find out.

New Mountains

If continents move, they eventually must bump into each other, and they do. Although it all happens over millions of years, the moving plates break and bend, causing earthquakes, volcanic eruptions and mountains to be pushed up.

That is why the limestones which formed as sediments and coral reefs under the sea are found on top of high mountain ranges. There they are worn away by wind and rain, releasing the carbon dioxide back into the atmosphere.

This process is speeded up by all the sulphur released from the volcanoes. When it rises into the air, it meets oxygen and forms sulphur dioxide. This dissolves in the clouds, making the rain acid.

Sulphur released into the sea is taken up by tiny floating plants which make oxygen and a smelly gas containing sulphur. This also meets oxygen in the atmosphere and helps to make more acid rain.

The acid in the rain also dissolves the rocks more rapidly, releasing the carbon dioxide and all the other minerals which have been locked up for millions of years.

Slightly acid rain is natural and a good thing because it keeps Spaceship Earth supplied with sulphur. All living things need sulphur to grow well. Natural acid rain helps to keep the Earth fertile.

Clean, White Poles

The North and South poles are very strange places. They each have very long summer days when there is no night, and six months of winter when the Sun never rises and it is dark all day. It is very cold at the poles, especially in the winters.

Island of Ice

The North pole is the middle of a large frozen sea which is about five times as big as the Mediterranean. Only the surface is frozen, to a depth of 10 feet (3 m.).

The North pole is surrounded by the continents of Europe, Asia and North America and the giant island of Greenland.

The Cold, Clean Mirror

While the Arctic Ocean at the North pole stays frozen and covered with clean, white snow, it acts like a giant mirror. It reflects much of the Sun's heat back into space, keeping Spaceship Earth cool.

Each summer, some of the ice melts and the deep blue sea absorbs the energy of the Sun. Water evaporates from the sea and clouds form.

If the Tides Comes In

If all the world's ice melted, it would pour down into the sea. Sea levels would rise by more than 100 feet (30 m.). The sea would flood vast areas of low land around the coasts and some major cities, such as New York, London and Tokyo.

More deep blue sea and warmer temperatures would mean more evaporation, more clouds and more snow on the mountains, so the ice caps could build up again.

Ice Ages

Only 20,000 years ago, the world was in the grip of the last ice age. Sheets of ice covered much of Scandinavia, northern Europe, Canada and the high mountain ranges of the world. Sea levels were lower then – so low that Britain was joined to Europe, and Alaska was joined to Russia.

Ice sheets change whole landscapes, carving out valleys and smashing up rocks. When the ice melts, there is lots of nice ground-up rock, full of minerals, ready for new soil to form.

More than 90% of all fresh water on Spaceship Earth is still locked up in the form of ice, on mountain tops and especially around the North and South poles.

Frozen Continent

Until 27 million years ago, Antarctica was still joined to South America, and warm water flowed from the Tropics toward the cold South pole. As the two continents separated, the cold polar waters circulated around Antarctica, sealing in the cold.

About 14 million years later, Antarctica was covered with ice. About 12 million years after that, the ice ages covered large parts of North America and Europe with sheets of ice.

The South pole is in the middle of a continent about $1\frac{1}{2}$ times the size of the U.S.A. It has great mountain ranges, covered with ice sheets, in places $1\frac{3}{4}$ miles (3 km.) thick.

There are billions of tons of ice pressing down on the land. If all the ice melted, the land would rise up so much that some of the Antarctic mountains would be taller than Mount Everest.

Fantastic Fact

Penguins in the Antarctic have heat exchangers in their legs to keep their feet warm. Warm blood from their bodies going down their legs, heats up the cold blood coming back from their feet. Penguins will sit on their tails, holding their feet up to the Sun to warm them.

17

The Human Crew Takes Charge

The very first members of the human crew appeared on Spaceship Earth about 3½ million years ago. They lived in the Great Rift Valley of Africa. They collected leaves, nuts, eggs and berries to eat and hunted the animals of the grasslands.

Small and weak compared with the big game they hunted, the humans only survived because they helped each other, living and working together in small family groups.

Upsetting the Balance

At first, there were not very many people at all. Then, as their numbers grew, they had to spread out to find enough food for the extra people. It happened slowly at first, over several billion years.

Up until then, all the different forms of life had played their part in keeping the life support systems in balance on Spaceship Earth. From this time on, people began to take charge.

People learned how to use fire. With it, they could clear land more easily and hunt animals. They used fire to cook their food and make it easier to eat.

The Farming Revolution

People made tools of flint, bones, polished stone, bronze and iron. With them, people could clear land. They began to grow crops and keep cattle, sheep, pigs and goats, as well as chickens, geese and ducks. This was the start of the farming revolution.

This was the time – at the end of the last ice age – when people began to spread across the world, crossing land which is now covered by the sea. The sea levels were much lower than they are today because so much water was locked up as ice sheets on the land.

The people colonized America and Australia and other parts of the world. The growing population needed more land to hunt and grow food and more space to live.

People started to control the environment more and more. They could grow and store food for the winter. They began to settle down and live in villages. The first civilizations were born in China, Egypt, India, Sri Lanka and South and North America.

The Industrial Revolution

Industry and transportation – at first powered by wind and water, and then, thanks to steam engines, by wood and then coal – began to change the world more rapidly. People started to live in towns and cities.

There were lots of new jobs to do in factories to earn a living. Fewer and fewer people farmed the land because the new farm machines could do the work more quickly. Pollution of rivers and the air became a fact of life and death. Diseases, such as bubonic plague, Black Death and cholera, swept through the crowded towns and cities.

The Scientific Revolution

The study of science led to a better understanding of the causes of disease and public health. Scientists now knew that people needed supplies of clean water and proper sewage systems to live healthy lives.

The population explosion had begun. People were in charge, or were they? Had they already lost control?

Extinction is for Ever

More than 5 billion people now live on Space Ship Earth. About 3 billion live in the poor Third World and more than l billion live in China. As you are reading this book, you are probably one of the rest – a first-class passenger from the rich First World.

To make room for us and supply us with all the things we need – and the greedy with all the things they want – forests, grasslands and wetlands have been destroyed. They are now being destroyed at the dreadful rate of 2½ acres every second of every day.

Dead as a Dodo

The symbol of extinction is the dodo. Its only home was on the island of Mauritius. Only 85 years after people first settled on the island and hunted with guns and dogs, all these large flightless birds had been wiped out. Dodos are thought to be a type of big pigeon.

When the Maori people first discovered New Zealand only about 900 years ago, it was the home of many flightless birds, some of them very large. Hunting, burning down the forests, and dogs soon destroyed them and much of their habitat.

As European settlers cut down more and more forest to grow crops, passenger pigeons became the commonest birds in the eastern states of the U.S.A. They were so common, they ate the farmers and animals out of house and home.

Perching in their thousands, it is said the pigeons snapped branches and toppled trees. By l923, they were extinct, probably because most of the forests in which they survived over the winter had been cut down. The Carolina parakeet also died out with them.

On the Danger List

Some scientists estimate that one in 10 of all the plants and animals that are alive today are on the danger list. Many of these are tiny insects, and most have not even been given a proper scientific name yet. Each one has an important job to do in the ecosystems in which they live. And they may well be useful to the human crew.

So far, we have looked at only about 1% of all the plants to see if they could be useful as medicines or in the manufacture of oils, resins and chemicals.

The Collectors

On land, everywhere we look, animals and birds -- pandas, chimpanzees, tigers, oryx, polar bears, penguins and walruses – are all under threat. The saddest part of all this is that the rarer the animals become, the more valuable they seem to be.

There is an enormous trade in wildlife, both alive and dead, because people want to collect rare animals and birds. This trade is said to be worth at least $100 million a year, although there is an international agreement, called CITES, which aims at stopping it.

Rare plants are also threatened by an international trade. Even where reserves are set up to protect them, people sneak in and dig up and sell the rarities.

Big Game

Stellar's sea cow was discovered in 1741, on the Aleutian Islands. It probably weighed up to 2¼ tons and fed on seaweed. Unfortunately, people found it was so good to eat that it was extinct 24 years later. If only Greenpeace had been around in those days!

How You Can Help

Make sure your backyard, school ground, local parks and even churchyards are wildlife friendly.

Support your local zoo. Good zoos are good news, but bad ones should be closed or made to mend their ways.

Support a national or international conservation body, such as World Wide Fund for Nature and Greenpeace.

Support your local wildlife group.

Never, ever buy souvenirs made of wild animals or parts of them. That includes corals and shells.

Saved, We Hope!

The cetaceans – the whales and dolphins of the world – are a group of wonderful animals. They would have been hunted to extinction by now if it wasn't for all the hard work of the conservation groups. The battle is not completely won yet. There is still an awful lot of work to do to save them.

The Spaceship Store

Spaceship Earth is like a giant supermarket. It has all the different kinds of plants which feed and help to shelter all the animals, including us. We get the energy our bodies use from this food. The plants get it from the Sun.

Wherever the weather is warm enough and there is enough water, all sorts of plants and animals live on the land. In the wettest, warmest parts, there are tropical rain forests. In the colder parts, there is the tundra, and in the hot and not too dry places there is semidesert. These are called ecosystems. They act like giant solar panels.

Sun and Soil

Each ecosystem, or solar panel, has layers of leaves, growing at different levels to trap as much Sun as possible. The leaves are held up by stems, trunks and branches. Roots reach down into the soil, tapping the supplies of water and minerals. Animals and fungi in the soil break down all the dead leaves, plants and animals that fall onto it and recycle the minerals.

Ecosystems are marvels of engineering. They grow by themselves, and they repair and maintain themselves, using only the energy of the Sun, water and minerals in the soil.

They can respond to changes in the climate, slowly moving up and down mountains (if the weather slowly grows warmer or colder) over several years.

During the last ice age, tundra covered much of Europe and the U.S.A., and the slopes of many mountains. As the weather grew warmer, at the end of the ice age, other ecosystems moved back to cover the land.

Spaceship Store

Here are just some of the things we get from the different areas of the world.

Do you know where any of the other foods you eat come from?
If so, add them to the right list.

Tropical Rain Forest: Rubber, lumber, lychees, coconuts, pineapples, bananas, brazil, macadamia and cashew nuts, pepper, cinnamon, cloves, nutmeg, cocoa, tea, coffee, tomatoes, sugar and chickens.

Semidesert: Melons, pumpkins, squashes, beans, sunflowers, artichokes and prickly pears.

Tundra: Potatoes, cranberries, blueberries, saffron and goats.

Wetlands: Rice, reeds for thatching and willow for basket making.

Deciduous Forest: Pecans, walnuts, chestnuts, hazelnuts, almonds, pears, apples, plums, cherries, oranges, lemons, raspberries, strawberries, red- and blackcurrants, grapes, gooseberries, pigs and turkeys.

Conifer Forest: Softwood lumber, pulp, pinewood and venison.

Grasslands: Corn, wheat, barley, sorghum, millet, rye, potatoes, sweet potatoes, endive, fennel, dill, cattle and horses.

Air Conditioners

During the day, plants take in carbon dioxide and use the energy of the Sun to make sugar. They also produce oxygen which goes into the atmosphere. At night, they use sugar and oxygen to produce carbon dioxide. They and the animals help to keep the gases of the atmosphere in balance.

Drugstore

Many modern medicines and drugs come from wild plants. Aspirin comes from willow trees and rozy periwinkle is used to help cure leukemia.

Tropical rain forests are a storehouse of drugs and medicines – a living medicine chest. Tubocurarine, which makes open-heart surgery possible, comes from a tropical liana. Reserpine, which makes eye operations possible, comes from a tropical plant.

Tropical Rain Forests - Solar Panel 1

The famous tropical rain forests grow in the warmest and wettest parts of the world. Here, it is very warm all the year around and it rains almost every day. The trees and plants grow well, producing masses of fruits and brilliantly colored flowers. These forests are home to more than half of all the different kinds of plants and animals on Spaceship Earth.

Rain Forest Facts

Rain forests once covered about 8 million square miles (13 million square kilometers) of Spaceship Earth – an area almost twice the size of Australia. Many millions of tribal people used to live in the rain forests without destroying them.

Destroying the Forests

People looked at the enormous trees and thought that the soil must be fantastically rich. They tried to set up massive farms. But when they cut down the trees, and burnt them, the recyclers had gone and the nutrients were soon washed away by the rain. With it went the homes of millions of plants, animals and people. After a few years, the farms soon failed and the people moved on to destroy more forest. Unfortunately, the destruction still goes on. It must stop.

Forest Lumber

Some of the best hardwood lumbers grow in the rain forests, woods such as mahogany, teak and ebony. They have been cut down for hundreds of years to make the best and most valuable furniture.

How You Can Help

When your family buys anything made of wood, try to make sure that the wood comes from forests that are properly managed – where young trees are planted to replace those that are cut down. For the next few years, this is going to be very difficult, but please try, for the sake of the forests.

The Tundra - Solar Panel 2

Far from the hot tropical rain forests are the colder regions – on the tops of mountains and near the poles. Here it is too cold for the trees to grow and the soil under the ground may be frozen all the year around. As soon as the ice melts in the summer, the plants do their best to grow, flower and produce seeds before the winter starts again.

Useful Camouflage

Sloths move about very slowly, eating fruit and spreading the seeds in their dung. Tiny blue-green plant-like organisms grow on their fur, making it look green. This acts as a camouflage for the sloths and hides them from their predators among the leaves. The blue-greens also take nitrogen from the air and help to keep the forest supplied with this important soil fertilizer.

The Recyclers

Leaf cutter ants are just one of millions of types of insects which help to recycle the nutrients, or plant food, and keep the forest soil fertile. The ants take pieces of leaf back to their nests and grow fungi on them to feed their young.

These fungi are part of the underground network of life in the soil. They help to break down all the dead leaves, branches, trees, fruit and even dead animals and birds which fall to the forest floor. They recycle all the nutrients in them directly back to the tree roots.

Winter Sleep

Animals which live in the tundra, such as grizzly bears, hibernate, or sleep, during the winter when there is not enough food to eat. In summer, they feed on everything that comes their way, such as fruits, honey, fish, fowl and meat.

To find enough food to eat, the grazing animals, such as caribou, reindeer and musk oxen, must keep on the move all the time.

Following the Herds

The people of Lapland have really come to terms with life on their part of the tundra. They migrate with their reindeer herds as they move in search of food. It is a cold, hard life but the Lapps live among some of the most spectacular landscapes in the world.

The Inuits, or Eskimos, as they are wrongly called, hunt the animals of the tundra for food and furs. Their way of life also depends on the sea and they fish alongside polar bears for seals, walruses and even whales.

The tundra makes up about 12% of the Earth's surface and much of it is still intact. But parts of it are being damaged by the search for oil and minerals, by the uncontrolled hunting of animals, by alpine skiing and atmospheric pollution.

Trees and Woodlands - Solar Panel 3

There are only 550 kinds of softwood trees – the kind of trees that have cones – on Spaceship Earth but they have a very important part to play. Many are evergreen and their needle-shaped leaves stay on the trees all the year around, ready to switch on and make sugar and oxygen whenever there is enough water and sunlight.

Useful Softwoods

Sitka spruce and other softwoods, which grow on the edge of the tundra, have special antifreeze in their sap so they do not freeze in winter. Their conical shape sheds snow so the branches are not broken by the weight.

Douglas fir and western hemlock trees thrive in the wettest, mild climates. These temperate rain forests are very productive. This is thanks to a complex of fungi living in the soil which pipe the minerals from all dead material back into the tree roots. They are also home to many endangered birds, such as northern spotted owls.

The giant and coast redwood trees of California are the biggest and the tallest living plants on Spaceship Earth. Many of the pines are resistant to fire, thanks to their thick bark which protects them. They are also resistant to drought.

Some of these softwood trees grow very fast and their lumber is useful for many things, including making paper. Much of the coniferous forests of Spaceship Earth have already been cut down at least once and many of their plants and animals are in danger.

Save Trees

Try to make sure that all the lumber in your home and garden is properly treated with wood preservative so that it lasts a long time. Check that the preservative is applied properly and is wildlife friendly, especially to bats.

Save Paper

By using recycled paper whenever possible.

By making sure there is a paper recycling program near your home and school.

When you go shopping, take a basket so you don't need a new bag.

Say "no" to goods with more layers of packaging than they really need.

Much of the land on which coniferous forests used to grow is now covered with fields, farms and towns. The animals and plants that were once common in the forests are now rare.

Broadleaf Woodlands

Broadleaf trees have flowers, fruits and nuts and many drop their leaves in the fall. Their leaves feed the worms and fungi in the soil, recycling the minerals. The spring Sun quickly warms the soil, producing a good crop of grasses and herbs to feed the animals after a long winter.

Nuts and fruits, such as pecans, hazelnuts, walnuts and crab apples, feed the animals and birds in the fall, ready for the winter again. The trees also produce the so-called hardwoods which, like those of tropical rain forests, are used to make beautiful furniture.

How You Can Help

Plant native trees in your backyard and school grounds but, remember, some of them do grow very large.

Support your local wildlife groups and help them with tree planting. Help with maintaining woodlands but, remember, this may include felling some mature trees and planting new ones.

Learn as much as you can about the trees of the world. They are of great importance to the future of Spaceship Earth's soils, wildlife and people.

Go out and hug a tree today!

Gum Trees and Forests

Gum, or eucalyptus, trees in Australia produce leaves for koalas to feed on and wonderful lumber. Many of Australia's other animals and plants also live in these eucalyptus forests.

Many types of gum tree can resist the forest fires, which are very common during the dry season. Some actually need fire to open up the gum nuts and release the seeds. The fires also clear the forest floor, providing space for new trees to grow. Gum trees are now being planted all over the world.

27

The Great Grasslands - Solar Panel 4

There are grasslands where there is not quite enough rain for thirsty trees – and they do need a lot of water – and wherever there are often fires in the dry season of the year.

Grasses are amazing plants. There are more than 9,000 different kinds. They cover and protect the soil, their matted roots binding and holding it together. Their leaves can be cropped again and again because they grow from near the base of the plant. Grasses provide plenty of food for animals – and a regular chore with the lawnmower!

Grassland Animals

The most famous grasslands are those in Africa. This is where many of the big game animals live. Many of the grazing animals migrate from the open grasslands to the dry forests at different times of the year.

Animals come in all shapes and sizes, from aardvarks living in the ground, to elephants and giraffes which get their food from the tallest parts of the trees. Lions, cheetahs, hyenas, eagles and vultures are some of Spaceship Earth's most spectacular recyclers.

Grassland or Food?

The main threat to these wonderful grasslands are people. Now that less and less people live by hunting the wild game, many more are clearing large areas to use as farmland.

Here is a very difficult problem. Much of the natural vegetation, in what are now the rich countries of the world, has been destroyed to grow food. Now the poor countries are saying, "We have the right to do the same."

How You Can Help

Never buy wildlife souvenirs of any sort. Only buy handcrafted local goods.

Support the local and international conservation associations in every way you can.

The Deserts - Solar Panel 5

Fires, started by lightning, burn at the beginning of the wet season. The ash from the fires releases nutrients into the soil, providing a new crop of young green grass for the animals.

Deserts are too hot and dry, or too cold for anything but tough and special plants to grow there. In some places, the plants and animals may have to survive for years without water. Any rain that does fall may be in a few stormy showers which quickly dry up in the hot Sun. The semideserts are Spaceship Earth's strangest and most exclusive solar panels.

Desert Plants

To conserve water, cacti and succulent plants open up their pores and take in carbon dioxide only in the cool of the night. It is stored as acid which is used up during the day to make sugar and oxygen.

Most of the animals come out at night and all of them have to be very careful not to get too hot. Other animals, such as jack rabbits and kit foxes, have large ears which help to cool them down.

After a shower of rain, seeds, which may have lain in the ground for many years, grow and flower very quickly, painting the desert with a riot of colors.

Frogs and toads emerge from underground retreats.

Semideserts are under attack from grazing animals and even the nature reserves are in danger from cactus rustlers who come to steal prize specimens.

Grasslands of America

The North American prairies and South American savannahs were once the home of huge herds of animals, which included mammoths, mastodons and saber-toothed tigers. They all died out – and not all that long ago. The only ones which lasted into more recent times were the bison. Sadly, these have nearly all gone, hunted almost to extinction. Their ranges and the lifestyles of the Indians have been replaced by cattle and sheep ranches, and by the largest cornfields in the world.

Vanishing Grasslands

The grasslands of Europe and Asia, some of which are cold and some are hot, were also the home to many wonderful plants and animals. Among them were wild horses and cattle, buffalo and, yes, even wolves, lions and rhinoceroses. Most of their habitats, and the homes of the wandering people who lived with them, have been replaced with farmland and towns.

How You Can Help

A cactus collection at home is your own desert reserve. Make sure you only buy them from good stores and not from cactus rustlers.

Wetlands, Past and Present - Solar Panel 6

Wherever fresh water flows from the tops of mountains down to the sea, there are wetlands. They are overflowing with life, such as fish, insects, snails, amphibians, water plants and birds.

Swamps and Marshes

In springs, streams and rivers, the flow of water is very fast. Only powerful swimmers and animals which can hang on or live under stones, can survive. In these places, there is plenty of oxygen in the water. Dead material quickly breaks down and is washed away.

In lakes, pools and ponds, the water flow is slower. More plants, water lilies, pond weeds, reeds and rushes can grow, slowing the flow of water even more. Eventually, the open water disappears and is replaced by reed swamps and marshlands.

Less and less water flow means less oxygen in the water. The dead remains of plants and animals begin to pile up as peat. At first, the peat is full of minerals brought in by the flowing water. This is called fen peat. Later, the peat gets poorer in minerals and becomes acid. This is called bog peat.

Acid boglands cover large areas of Spaceship Earth. The biggest of them are in the wet, cool regions and along the coasts in the wettest parts of the Tropics.

Each type of wetland has its own special plants and animals. Birds fly in from all over the world to rest and nest in the safety of these wet wonderlands.

Wetlands in Danger

All the world's wetlands are under threat. The swamps, marshes and mineral-rich peats are being drained and used for farming. Draining the peat opens it up to oxygen in the air and it soon decays away.

The acid peats are also being drained and the peat harvested to produce gas and potting compost.

Ancient methods of digging peat with shovels were slow and did not cause too much damage. Modern methods, using giant machines, are large scale, rapid and very destructive.

Wetland Facts

Russia has 70 power stations running on peat, using 71½ million tons of peat every year.

If all the peat in the world was opened up to the air or burned, it would release 560 billion tons of carbon dioxide into the atmosphere.

In England, only 2% of the lowland bogs now remain in a more or less natural state.

In Great Britain, more and more bogs are being drained and planted with conifers.

How You Can Help

Never buy peat to use in your garden. Many peat substitutes are now on sale and you can make your own compost in a compost heap.

Wetlands of the Past

Before the dinosaurs roamed Spaceship Earth, enormous areas of land were covered with wetlands. Large tree-like ferns, club mosses and horsetails, grew on them, some as much as 130 feet (40 m.) high.

When these plants fell into the swampy oxygen-poor water, their remains formed peat on a massive scale. The Carboniferous, or coal-forming, period lasted for 65 million years. During this time the peat was compressed and turned to coal.

Unfortunately, the Carboniferous period was also a time of great volcanic activity. Sulphur from the volcanoes near the coal swamps was trapped in the peat. Because of this, some of the coal has a lot of sulphur in it. Coal is Spaceship Earth's most plentiful form of fossil fuel. When it is burned, it puts a lot of sulphur into the atmosphere.

Where Does All Your Food Come From?

Does your food come from the supermarkets? Yes. Does it come from all over the world? Yes. (Look on the back of the food cans and packages). Does your food come from the soil? Yes. And that's the most important of all.

Soil, People and Food

Soil is made of mineral particles of the rocks which have been broken down by rain, frost, plant roots and burrowing animals, such as worms.

The waste from all the plants and animals which live on or in the soil help to glue the mineral particles together. This gives the soil a crumb-like structure through which water can drain and air can circulate.

In the wettest parts of the world, if too much water drains through the soil, it washes out all the minerals and the soil becomes acid.

In the drier parts of the world, if too much water evaporates from the surface, the soil can become salty and alkaline.

Farmers must try to keep the soil well balanced. They must also replace the nitrates, phosphates and all the other mineral nutrients that are removed with each crop. Only then can they grow good crops and help to feed you and keep you healthy.

Growing Crops

At first, the farmers used lots of human and animal manure to keep the soils full of organic material and fertilizer.

Later, farmers grew different crops each year on one piece of land. This is called crop rotation. They planted beans and peas one year. These have nodules containing bacteria which fix nitrogen from the atmosphere and make fertilizer in the soil. The next year, they grew cereals which used up the nitrogen and provided lots of straw. The third year, they let the soil rest, grazing animals on the weeds. Manure from the animals helped the soil.

Guano Islands

Farmers later used imported fertilizers. At first supplies of fertilizer came from the coast of Peru. Fleets of sailing ships braved the stormy waters of Cape Horn to reach the Guano Islands on the desert coast of Peru.

The cold waters around the coast are full of nutrients which well up from deep in the ocean. They provide the world with its best fishing grounds and the anchovies many of us like on our pizzas.

For thousands of years, millions of sea birds have eaten the anchovies and other fish, and covered the islands where they nest with their droppings. These droppings, called guano, are a rich organic fertilizer. All the ships had to do was load it up and sail back home, where they sold the guano to farmers for their crops.

Food from the World

Find out where all the food you eat in a week comes from. Look on the backs of the packages, cans and jars in your kitchen. Check the boxes and trays of fruit and vegetables when you next go to your local supermarket.

It makes you feel important, doesn't it? You sit in the middle of a huge food web which covers the whole world.

These supplies are not enough for the modern world. Today, farmers plant enormous fields with the same crop year after year. To produce large crops, they have to add enormous quantities of fertilizers – potassium, nitrogen and phosphorous.

The potassium is dug from mines, and there are a lot of them around the world.

Nitrogen fertilizers are made in enormous factories which take the nitrogen from the atmosphere. As long as there are enough fossil fuels to drive the factories, the supply of nitrogen is safe.

Phosphorous is mined in different parts of the world. But so much of it is being used up that supplies could run out in the next century.

33

Animal Rights and Human Wrongs

Scientists working in research laboratories have invented new medicines, antiseptics, vaccines and antibiotics. They help to control many killer diseases, such as malaria, cholera, yellow fever, smallpox and typhoid.

New Medicines

The scientists soon realized that the new cures for the diseases had to be tested to make sure they were safe before they could given to people. They decided to carry out many of the tests on animals, such as rats and mice, and even cats, dogs, marmosets, monkeys and chimpanzees.

Some people argue that this is all right, as long as the tests are really necessary. And that the work is done by professional, caring people who obey all the rules laid down by the government.

Other people strongly disagree and say that we have no right to treat animals in this way. Most people now agree that using animals to test cosmetics and household goods is wrong.

There is more good news on the way because scientists are now able to do many of the tests on cell cultures in laboratories, not on live animals.

What You Can Do to Help

Always buy cosmetics and household goods which bear the label, "Not tested on animals."

Animals for Food

Vegetarians – people who do not eat animal products – argue that eating meat is very wasteful. It takes a lot more land to raise a crop of meat than to grow a crop of cereal or beans.

People who eat meat point out that we cannot digest grass, so why don't we let the animals do it for us? We can eat the meat, milk, yogurt, butter and cheese. And, to plant crops, we must plow the land. This can lead to soil erosion, especially on the poorer soils where the animals usually graze.

People are beginning to agree that growing cereals on good land to feed cattle is a waste.

Animal Furs

Until quite recently, many people longed to own a fur coat. They gave little thought to how the animals were caught and killed. Farms of mink, chinchilla and Arctic fox boosted the supply of valuable furs.

Some people campaigned that it was wrong to trap such beautiful wild animals, let alone breed them in tiny cages, just for vanity. Today, thanks to these people, fur coats are no longer as popular. Many new and beautiful synthetic furs look just as good and are as warm.

But what about the problem of leather coats, belts and shoes, and killing animals for food?

Some people say we have the right to kill animals as long as no cruelty is involved. Others say no animal should be killed to provide us with anything at all.

Difficult Decisions

These are called "ethical decisions" which we must all make for ourselves. Think carefully. Would you eat meat or wear a leather coat if you had to kill the animals yourself?

Other decisions are easier. Eggs laid by chickens kept in open fields cost more than those raised in tiny cages in sheds. The same is true for all animals raised in a less intensive way. We should be willing to pay the extra costs to make sure that the animals we make use of live as pleasant and as natural lives as possible.

Should we kill animals at all? Rats, which eat huge amounts of food on our farms, must be controlled. How about mice and cockroaches in our homes? And what do you do with the spider in the bath, that annoying bluebottle, wasps, biting midges and disease-carrying mosquitoes? Where do animal rights stop?

Ethical decisions are very difficult but they are very important. We all have to make up our minds for ourselves.

Personal Problems

Every day we go to the bathroom to clean our teeth, take a bath and to do other very personal things. All the food we can't digest is called organic waste. This contains lots of chemicals and minerals which go down the pipes and end up in our local rivers.

We also like to keep our houses, clothes, sports gear and cars clean. To do this, we use lots of water and chemical detergents, many of which contain lots of phosphate. This also goes down the drain.

Waste Problems

Organic waste in the rivers is broken down by bacteria which use oxygen. If there is too much organic waste, the bacteria use up all the oxygen dissolved in the water. Without oxygen, the fish, insect and much of the other water life die, adding to the problem.

Sewage works remove much of the solid matter from the organic waste. This is then dumped, often in the sea, where it causes the same sort of problem.

Fantastic Fact

About 40% of all the phosphate causing problems in British rivers comes from detergents.

Unfortunately, most of the minerals, such as phosphates and nitrates, are plant foods. They pass through the sewage works and into the rivers. There they can cause the water plants to grow out of control. When the plants die and decay, bacteria use up all the oxygen in the water, killing all the other water life.

Down to the Sea

All these minerals are on trip to the sea. On the way, they flow through the estuary, or mouth, of a river.

There they can cause the same sort of problems. Too much blanket weed grows on the surface of the mud, making it impossible for the wading birds to feed. When the weed dies and decays, it can use up the oxygen in the mud. Then the animals living in the mud cannot survive.

In the past, most coastal towns simply poured their sewage into the sea. This problem became worse in the vacation season when many people stayed in the hotels and swam in the sea.

Unfortunately, this is still true in many places. Long pipes have been built to carry sewage out to sea but this is not the answer. It should be treated first to remove organic matter, bacteria and viruses which could cause diseases.

Even then, the nutrients, all that precious phosphate and nitrate, flow on into the sea.

Poisonous Blooms

Once in the sea, the nutrients help the plankton to multiply and grow to plague proportions, called blooms. The growth is so great that the sea becomes like tomato ketchup and at night it glows with phosphorescence.

Poisons from these blooms get into seafood, such as mussels and oysters, and can kill the people who eat them.

Other plankton in the sea recycle the sulphur in the sewage. They release it into the air and help to make the rain more acid.

Flushing away our personal waste may be easy but the problems it causes from then on are enormous. And, remember, the fertilizers we need to grow our food, especially phosphates, are expensive and in very short supply.

How You Can Help

We can't stop going to the bathroom but we can all use phosphate-free detergents and soaps.

Always use biodegradable cleaners and, of course, avoid all cleaning and toilet products which have been tested on animals.

Always run washing machines and dishwashers with full loads.

Watery Dumping Ground

Every day frost, ice, snow, rain and wind scrape a billion tons of earth, silt and mud off the land and dump it in the sea. This is all part of a natural process called erosion. It helps to keep the sea around the coasts rich in mineral food which feeds all the sea creatures, including fish, whales and dolphins.

Speeding It Up

People speed up this process of erosion. Together we dump an extra 29 billion tons every day into the sea. This includes a lot of very precious soil as well as poisonous chemicals, oil, radioactive waste, sewage, plastics and garbage. In the sea, it may poison and kill the sea creatures.

Large herds of cows produce large amounts of manure. There may be too much to spread on the land as fertilizer. Rain running off heaps of manure may poison fish in the streams.

The rain also washes soil from building sites, and oil and trash from the streets into the drains and down to the sea.

Many factories take huge amounts of water from rivers. The water they put back into the rivers can contain poisonous chemicals and factory waste.

Where forests are cut down, rain and wind sweep away the soil. Much of it ends up in the rivers.

How You Can Help

When you are on the beach, take all your trash home with you. Be careful not to let trash, especially plastic bags, blow away in the wind.

Help by collecting trash on beaches, especially anything made of plastic. Take it home and put it in a trash can. Plastic takes hundreds of years to rot away.

Don't be tempted to throw garbage overboard when you are on a boat or a ship. Find a trash can or take it home. You may save the life of a bird or some other sea creature.

Oil tankers wash out their tanks at sea, although it is now against the law. They also have accidents and may spill huge amounts of oil which end up on the coasts.

Oil terminals and refineries on the coasts sometimes have accidents which spill oil into the sea. Every year 224,000 tons of oil leak from the pipes and storage tanks.

Ships carry factory waste and human sewage sludge out to sea where it is dumped away from the coasts.

Radioactive nuclear waste in sealed drums has been dumped into very deep parts of the oceans. But the drums may leak, releasing dangerous radiation into the sea.

Sometimes factories also accidentally spill chemicals, some very poisonous, from tanks on the riverbanks.

Danger in the Sea

Over 2 million sea birds are killed every year by spilled oil and by eating the garbage in the sea. More than 100,000 marine animals, including seals, whales and dolphins, die every year from eating garbage, especially plastic.

Turtles die after swallowing plastic bags, thinking they are jellyfish. A dead sperm whale had dozens of plastic bags in its stomach.

Farmers use chemicals on their land to grow bigger crops, and to kill pests and weeds. Some of the chemicals seep through the ground to the rivers.

Fish die when the water is poisoned with chemicals. Some chemicals cause so many bacteria to grow in the water that they use up all the oxygen in it and the fish die.

39

Mountains of Trash

Every year, each one of us living in the rich countries of the world throws away over half a ton of trash. We throw away drink cans and bottles, newspapers and magazines, all the paper and plastic packaging food comes in, lots of stale food, masses of garden waste and huge amounts of other garbage.

Dangerous Trash

Some of this trash is burned, putting dust and dirt into the air as well as the greenhouse gases. Most of it is dumped in holes in the ground, such as old quarries, gravel pits and mines, and even in natural valleys where it smothers the wildlife.

As the trash rots, it may pollute the springs, streams and rivers. It also produces a gas called methane. This is a greenhouse gas which can, and does, cause explosions.

New Cans for Old

We now know that we can get rid of all this trash in a proper way. Aluminum and tin cans can be recycled into new cans. This saves the coal or oil used to make the cans in the first place, and reduces the amount of tin and aluminum that has to be mined and quarried.

Paper can be recycled to make new paper so we don't have to chop down so many trees.

Some of the plastic can be used to make new bottles and even fence posts. The rest of the plastic cartons and containers can be made into pellets and burned in special incinerators to produce electricity.

All the organic waste – that is, grass cuttings, hedge trimmings, waste food and really soiled paper – can be made into compost. This can be used to grow crops in gardens and farms, and even to help reclaim deserts.

If we get rid of our trash in the right way, we save energy – coal, oil, gas and electricity. We save the world's resources of metals and slow down the destruction of natural habitats, such as the rain forests. We also reduce pollution and the release of greenhouse gases.

How You Can Help

If you have a backyard, persuade everyone in your house to put vegetable and fruit parings and scraps of food in a bucket lined with newspaper. This can be emptied on to the compost heap.

Plastic bags and cartons can be used over and over again for wrapping up food, storing and freezing food, and for taking food on picnics.

Find out if there is a local collection of waste paper in your area. Ask your family and friends to save all the clean paper they can.

Keep all glass bottles and jars in three boxes, one for clear glass, one for green and one for brown glass. When they are full, ask your family or friends to help you take them to your local bottle bank, if you have one. Cans and scrap metal can be recycled, too.

Fantastic Facts

It takes about six trees to make the paper each one of us in the rich world throws away every year.

Every ton of recycled waste glass saves energy – about equal to 30 gallons (135 liters) of oil.

Recycling aluminum cans saves up to 90% of the energy needed to mine and make new aluminum.

High-tech Pollution

In the modern high-tech world, factories making all the things we use and take for granted, such as toys, clothes, VCRs, computers, cars and even our food, produce lots of poisonous waste.

Cyanide is used to make steel, mercury is put into thermometers, chromium is used in plating works, cadmium in batteries and chlorine in bleaches. All these poisons are found naturally in the rocks of Spaceship Earth but when they are released into the soil, the air or the water, they can be killers.

Poisonous Chemicals

Industry produces many chemicals which are poisonous, either on purpose to do important jobs or as a by-product. If they escape in the soil, air or water, they can cause problems.

Many have long and complex names so we use initials. DDT and other pesticides, produced in the 1950s, had to be banned because of the damage they caused to wildlife. Unfortunately, some are still being used. CFCs are used in some refrigerators, aerosols, air conditioners and foam plastics.

Recently, it was found that when CFCs are released into the air, they rise high in the atmosphere. There they threaten to destroy the ozone layer which protects us from harmful rays from the Sun. Already there are signs that more people are suffering from sunburn and skin cancer.

PCBs, like CFCs, contain chlorine and have been widely used in the plastics and electricity industries. Recently, they have been found to be poisonous in very small amounts. Some scientists believe that if they go on leaking into the sea, whales and dolphins may not be able to produce healthy babies.

All these chemicals have been banned and must be got rid of safely. But how? Scientists say that burning them at very high temperatures would do the job. But who wants a poisonous waste incinerator in their backyard? Others say, store it all until scientists have invented a way to deal with it. But who wants a store of poisonous chemicals built near his or her house?

Dangerous Dumps

In the past and even today, much of the poisonous waste from industry is dumped, untreated, in old quarries and down mines. Some goes into valleys and even into the sea.

Just how many such dumps there are around the world waiting to be cleaned up is hard to guess. They must all be found and made safe. That is going to cost a lot of money. Thank goodness there are now specialists who are attempting to do just that.

How You Can Help

Lead was put in gasoline to help car engines to run smoothly. Lead is no longer necessary and many cars now use lead-free gas. Make sure your family car is lead free.

Buy rechargeable batteries or, better still, solar-powered calculators and toys.

Don't use CFC aerosols or packaging. Make sure your old refrigerators are disposed of properly by experts.

Never put plastics on the fire. Send them away for recycling.

If there are not any recycling schemes near your home, why not get your parents or teachers to help you to write to the local authorities and find out why?

Fantastic Facts

At Minamata Bay in Japan, over 400 people died from eating fish which had been poisoned by mercury leaked into the sea by a chemical factory.

Industry produces 370 million tons of poisonous and dangerous waste every year.

Burning Up the Future

In the rich countries of the world, we burn fossil fuels – coal, oil and natural gas – in vast quantities. We use these fuels to make electricity, to keep our houses warm or cool, to cook our food and to manufacture all sorts of things. We use oil to drive our cars, buses and trucks, and for farm machinery for growing food.

Many people in the Third World still use wood as a fuel for cooking and for heating. Wood is one form of solar power and it is renewable, as long as we have enough land and enough fertilizers to grow it.

Trees for Fuel

Unfortunately, 2 billion people are already cutting down trees for firewood faster than the trees can grow. As the world's stocks of fertilizers begin to run out, they become more and more expensive. The poor people cannot afford to use fertilizers to grow food crops, let alone to grow trees for firewood.

Fantastic Fact

Many people have to walk as much as 9 miles (14 km) every day just to gather the firewood they need.

When all the local firewood has been used, many people burn animal dung to cook their meals. That means less fertilizer to put on their land to grow food.

Growing Food

Long ago in the rich countries, the only energy people used to farm the land was their own muscle power and the muscle power of animals. They got their energy and minerals from the food they grew in the soil and their wastes were recycled back into the soil to fertilize it.

Now all that has changed. To feed the increasing number of people, we are burning more and more fossil fuels, to drive farm machinery, to work mines and to make more fertilizers and farm chemicals.

We also use vast amounts of energy to store, refrigerate, package and transport food around the world.

Burning Fossil Fuels

The fossil fuels were formed millions of years ago. When they are used up, they cannot be replaced. They are nonrenewable and are gone forever.

It is not wise just to burn them when they are needed for other things. Fossil fuels are the main raw material for the manufacture of plastics and chemicals. Once they have all been used up, we will have to grow more wood, cotton, silk and flax to take their place. Where will all the land, the energy and the fertilizers come from?

Burning fossil fuels produces carbon dioxide and other greenhouse gases. Some scientists believe that we are now burning them so fast that the Earth could be warming up. We can only guess what the result will be.

The worst result could be massive droughts in the main food growing areas and the spread of deserts. The sea levels could rise, flooding many of our major cities and much good farm land.

Burning fossil fuels also puts sulphur and nitrogen into the air, making the rain more acid.

Over large areas of the world, trees are dying and so are the fish and other life in the lakes and rivers.

These are enormous worldwide problems but we can all help by saving energy.

How You Can Help

You can save energy in lots of ways.

Always wear extra clothes indoors instead of turning up the heating.

Make sure that your house is well insulated.

If you can, always walk to school and home again. Bicycling is just as good.

Whenever you can, go by bus or train. If you do go by car, make sure that it is full of people.

All cars should use lead-free gasoline, or they should be fitted with the latest fuel-efficiency and exhaust-cleaning devices.

Replanting the Future

A lot of damage has already been done to Spaceship Earth. We must now stop any further destruction of the forests, the grasslands, the wetlands and the tundra. Then we must put the solar panels and life support systems back into working order.

All the world's national parks, nature reserves and wildlife sanctuaries must be made safe for the future. Money must be found to look after and protect them. The local people who live in them should be allowed to continue their own sustainable ways of life.

New Forests and Plantations

Large areas around the main wildlife reserves should be planted with a full variety of the local trees. The special plants, which provide food and raw materials for the people that live there, should also be planted.

Around these new forests, belts of fast-growing trees could be planted which would produce high-quality lumbers. Selected trees would be carefully cut down, so that they would not disturb or damage the other trees.

Craftsmen would make furniture and other high-quality wooden goods for sale.

The local people could work as rangers and wardens of the areas. They could also collect natural products, such as nuts, fruits, gums, resins and medicines, for local and other markets. These areas would also provide habitats for wild animals.

Plantations could also produce such things as palm oil, coconuts, bananas, cocoa and coffee. These could be sold for export, helping the government to earn money.

Visiting tourists would also be a source of international income.

Planting More Trees

The deserts on Spaceship Earth are growing bigger every year. To stop them growing and to make them smaller, millions and millions of trees must be planted. They must be the right trees in the right place. They must also be looked after and protected from grazing animals, both wild and domestic.

As the tree crops grew, they would take in carbon dioxide from the air. They would shade the ground from the Sun, cool the air and bind the soil on to the land. Farms between the plantations would grow a variety of food for the local people.

In this way, reserves, forests, plantations and farms could go on producing for ever and ever. But it must all be done very carefully.

In Africa, the green belt movement is helping to do this. The women and children go out and collect tree seeds. They raise them in nurseries and then plant the young trees in wide belts around their villages.

Good News

When old rubber trees stopped producing latex, which is made into rubber, they were burned. Now they are carefully felled and the wood made into furniture.

Wetlands can also be restored or renewed by blocking drains and building dams. But care must be taken because mosquitoes and other disease-carrying creatures breed on still water.

Too Many Animals

Some very sad decisions also have to be made. Animals, such as wildebeest and elephants used to roam over enormous areas. Now they are enclosed in parks and reserves. If there are too many animals, they destroy the vegetation.

If they wander outside the parks and reserves, they destroy farm crops. Some animals must be killed to stop this happening. Some people say that this should be done by big game hunters who pay to shoot the animals. Others say it should be done by paid government officials. Others say that no animals should be killed at all. How about you? What do you think?

This problem happens in other places. In Scotland, there are too many deer. Who should kill them? Should it be huntsmen who pay or estate managers who are paid? If nothing is done, many deer will die of starvation.

Possums and rabbits were introduced into New Zealand so that they could to be hunted for their fur. They have bred so well that there are now 100 million possums. They are destroying the forests, national parks and nature reserves. They must be controlled. It's sad but it's true.

47

Recycling Our Resources

All the vegetation on Spaceship Earth keeps on growing by recycling the water, carbon dioxide, oxygen and minerals. In the future, we shall have to do the same.

Nutrients are far too valuable to send on a one way trip down the drains and rivers to the sea. Scientists are inventing new ways of recycling sewage and other useful waste.

Sewage and Straw

Sewage is a valuable source of organic matter, energy, phosphate and other minerals.

Waste straw from farms used to be burned on the fields. It can now be collected and taken to a large concrete yard with drains around the edge. Sewage brought by tanker is sprayed on to the straw which absorbs it, like a huge diaper.

The straw is then heaped up into long rows under a roof, mixed at intervals, and left to compost. Bacteria work away, breaking down the sewage and straw. They work so hard that the temperature rises to 175°F (80°C), killing off all weed seeds and diseases. Seventeen days later, the straw can be spread on the farmers' fields as good organic fertilizer.

This stops the problems of sewage in the rivers and sea. The phosphate and other minerals go back on the land, which saves more being mined. The organic matter improves the soil structure and feeds bacteria, which make nitrogen fertilizer.

Fertilizer and Gas

Cow dung, collected as stockyard slurry, is pumped into closed tanks. There it is digested by special bacteria, which need no oxygen. They break down the sewage solids, producing methane gas. The methane is burned for heating on the farm and even to produce electricity. The liquid that is left in the tanks is rich in nutrients and is put back on the fields.

By early in the next century, all the electricity used in homes in Northern Ireland could be generated in this way.

Farmers in many countries raise enormous numbers of pigs and poultry. The slurry and dung from these animals is a real problem.

One way to solve the problem is to pump the organic matter into pools and let it stand. Plants, such as water hyacinths which are grown on the surface of the pools, take out much of the nutrients. The whole mass is then harvested and put in closed tanks. Here it produces methane, which is used as a fuel. What remains is a good organic fertilizer.

Burning Paper

Dirty paper and cardboard can be burned and the energy used for heating schemes and even to generate electricity. The rest can be composted in tall towers, producing soil conditioners.

Working Wetlands

New wetlands are being set up and planted with reed mace, bulrushes and reeds. Various types of liquid waste are piped into them. The poisons and nutrients are stripped out by the growing plants. These new working wetlands make great habitats for wildlife, especially waterfowl. The rushes and reeds can be used for fuel and even for thatching roofs.

Future Power - Wind, Water and Sun

We all use lots of power every day, mostly in the form of electricity. When you switch on a light, a heater or a television set, you use some of that electricity. Every year, everyone in the world wants more power for cooking, heating, lighting and all the electrical gadgets they would like to own.

Much of the electricity is produced by burning oil, coal or gas in power stations. One day, these fuels will all be used up. But there are others ways of making electricity, thanks to the wind, water and the Sun. These renewable forms of energy will last for ever.

Wind Power

Scientists are designing modern windmills, called aerogenerators, which produce electricity. They come in all shapes and sizes, from small units for single homes to giant ones which will supply whole communities with all the power they need. There are also wind farms feeding electricity into national and international power supply systems.

Whirling wind vanes, even very well designed ones, do have problems. They are not very beautiful things and will spoil landscapes and horizons. They are also very noisy and the whirling blades kill birds.

Wind farms with hundreds, or even thousands, of aerogenerators, will be needed. Where will they be built?

They could be put on sand banks and islands far out at sea, where they will be out of sight of land. Some could replace lighthouses, warning boats of shallow water. Their foundations will form artificial reefs, which will be good news for the marine life. The sails and vanes of the aerogenerators will have bright patterns on them so that they are seen by migrating birds.

Water power

One way of providing a cheap, renewable power supply is to use water running over dams to make electricity, or hydroelectricity.

The problem is that big dams cost a lot of money. They flood large areas of land upstream, destroying the homes of plants and animals and of local people.

Dams also hold back the silt in the water, which is rich in nutrients. Silt is a free fertilizer for water meadows, fish, wild life, and for farmers downstream.

The other problem is that still water can be a breeding ground for all sorts of water weeds, insects and diseases.

These problems must be thought about before new dams are designed and built.

Future hydroelectric systems will be on a smaller scale, using turbines built underwater in the rivers. Then there will be no need for large dams and the power of the water can be used again and again.

Wave Power

Generators using the waves to make electricity will also come in all shapes and sizes. Small units, like wide chimneys, will be built just under the water along sea cliffs and will work all the time. Inside each chimney will be a small turbine, turned by a wave as it goes up and comes down again.

Another design is called nodding ducks. Rafts of small floats, each one like a very badly designed boat, pitch and toss on the waves. These movements work small turbines inside each one.

Storms will be a real danger, threatening to smash the wave generators to pieces. There is also the problem that anything floating on the sea will make a home for animals and plants. The last thing you want your wave power plant to do is disappear inside a block of coral!

Some systems will use both wind and water power. Wind power will pump water from a river up into a series of reservoirs. They will act like batteries, storing the water until it is needed to turn the water turbines.

In Wales, there is a large hydro system built inside a hollowed out mountain. During the night, when there is not much demand for electricity, water is pumped back up the mountain. It can then be used again during the daytime.

Direct Solar Power

Lean-to conservatories built on to the side of a house will waft the warmth of the Sun into the house, even in winter. In summer, the fanlights and windows will allow the hot air to rise, drawing cool breezes through the house.

This type of solar heating uses no energy. It can be speeded up by a heat pump to move warm air from where it is not wanted to where it is wanted. In this way, houses can be heated or cooled by using very little extra energy.

More complicated types of solar heating consist of solar cells which turn the Sun's energy directly into electricity. These are costly but useful in sunny places.

Scientists have suggested that giant solar dishes could be put in orbit around the Earth. They would beam concentrated solar energy from space to the Earth.

The simplest kind of solar heating is a coiled piece of black hose, lying in the Sun. Try it for yourself, but be careful. It can get very hot. Cats will love it on sunny days in winter.

Future Power - Tides and Atoms

As well as wind power and wave power, the power of the tides is the most promising form of energy that could be developed. Tidal mills have been used to grind corn and work machinery for hundreds of years.

The problem is that dams, or barrages, must be built across the estuaries, or mouths, of rivers to send the tides flowing through the turbines. This will cause changes to the estuaries, both above and below the barrages.

Life in the Estuaries

Estuaries have important jobs to do. They are the feeding grounds for millions of birds and the spawning grounds for fish and shellfish. Many are already badly polluted and a barrage would make things worse. So they must be designed and built with extreme care.

Barrages have great potential because power can be generated as the tide runs in and out, all day and all night.

Energy Undergound

Countries such as Iceland, New Zealand and Italy have areas of volcanic activity. Bore holes in the ground can reach down and tap the hot water and steam deep under the ground. This is called geothermal power and is used to heat houses and drive turbines to make electricity.

Even where there are no active volcanoes and hot springs, there are hot rocks deep down in the Earth. Cold water is pumped down a deep bore hole and comes back much warmer up a second bore hole. But this form of geothermal energy is very expensive and has many problems.

Power from the Atom

Everything in the universe is made of tiny atoms. Within each atom there are tremendous amounts of energy, the energy which holds all things together.

There are two ways of getting at this energy. One is by splitting the atom, or fission, and releasing the energy in a very controlled way. The other way is by joining two atoms together, or fusion, and catching the spare energy.

Nuclear power stations do not produce greenhouse gases but they do produce dangerous radioactive waste. This must be got rid of in a safe way and looked after properly. It will be thousands of years before some of it is safe. This costs a lot of money.

The first atom-splitting power station started to produce electricity in Scotland in 1956. Today, there are more than 426 atomic power stations dotted around the world, supplying 17% of its energy.

Unfortunately, nuclear power stations can leak radiation and there is evidence that such leaks cause a higher rate of cancer in people living near them. They can, and do, have accidents, as the explosion at Chernobyl, in the Ukraine, proved in 1986.

They also cost an awful lot of money to build, to run and to safeguard. A number of countries and electricity companies have said "no" to this form of power production.

Fusion Power

Fusion power is the other hope and experiments are going on in several countries. Even the experimental power plants are enormous, very complicated and very expensive. The fusion reactions will only take place at very high temperatures, as high as the temperatures on the surface of the Sun. But, thank goodness, this type of nuclear power station will not leak radioactivity.

Scientists now think that we may get power from this source in about 40 years' time. The whole world must keep its fingers crossed because by then we will be desperate for more cheap, safe energy. So we must all do our part and save as much electricity as we can.

Fantastic Fact

If we insulate our houses and factories so that they lose the minimum amount of heat, and use all the fossil fuels with the maximum efficiency, it would save 60% of all the energy used by the rich countries.

Electric Cars

By the beginning of the next century, no cars burning gasoline or natural gas will be allowed in certain areas of California. This is to try to reduce air pollution and especially the very harmful chemical smog. Electric cars will be used instead.

This, of course, only solves the local problem because the electricity must be generated somewhere else.

Future Cities

By the end of this century, more than 60% of all the people in the world will live in towns and cities. The countryside will be somewhere they visit during their leisure time, if they want to, sort of like a wildlife park.

Going Underground

More and more parts of towns, especially in the colder climates, will be built underground. Such places as shopping malls, warehouses, industrial parks, cinemas, and indoor sports centers will always be warm, well lit and air conditioned.

Offices and houses will probably stay above the ground. Elevators will bring workers up to surface cafeterias and leisure rooms.

High-rise Villages

There will be a nucleus of high-rise condos, built like villages around parkland and nature reserves. These will provide green space for everyone, including the local wildlife.

We may not like the idea of high-rise and row houses, with lots of people living around shared facilities, such as swimming pools, sports centers, gardens and parks. But they do make a lot of sense. They cut down the need to travel and the loss of heat, especially when district heating comes from burning trash or methane from sewage.

An apartment surrounded by other apartments is well insulated on one, two, three or even four sides.

No More Cars

Public transportation and railroads will replace cars for all journeys in the cities. Bicycle and walkways will form green lanes, linking the whole city together.

Floating Towns

Whole floating towns are now being designed. They could be taken to offshore areas to house large numbers of workers for short periods. They would be totally self-contained with solar and wind power providing much of the energy. All waste water would be treated and purified before being returned to the sea.

Try designing your own city of the future. How and where would you like to live?

Crowded Cities

Hong Kong already has some of the features of a future city. More than 6 million people live in the city, close to their work, stores, sports and entertainment. This is thanks to one of the most efficient public transportation systems in the world.

Hong Kong also has some immense problems, such as pollution of the sea and air, and noise pollution from machinery which keeps the whole place working. These problems can be solved but how many people would choose to live like that? Would you?

High-tech Villages

In the future, some people will live in small villages and carry on their international businesses by fax and television satellite hook-up meetings. They will not need to commute to work every day, saving fuel and traffic jams.

55

Feeding the Crew

By the end of this century, there will be almost 7 billion people on Spaceship Earth. To feed them all, we will have to make huge changes in the way we grow our food.

Organic Farming

In the future, there will certainly be organic gardens and smallholdings, which do not use chemicals but use only natural fertilizers. But to return to a completely organic way of farming brings all sorts of problems.

Large fields full of one sort of crop are very likely to get diseases and to be eaten by pests. These diseases and pests are now controlled by chemicals. Without the chemicals, the crops would get the diseases and produce very much less food.

Modern chemical farming produces much more food from an area of land than organic farming, so it should also leave more space for other things, such as woodlands and wildlife. Organic farming would require more land to grow the same amount of food.

The way ahead is a mixture of the best of the old ways with the best of the new.

Crops without Soil

One way to produce more food is by growing crops using no soil at all. The plants grow in water with special chemicals supplying all the plant food. The water can be recycled and topped up with more nutrients. This is called hydroponics.

Hydroponics could be useful in countries where irrigation water is too precious to spray on crops, or where the soil becomes salty due to evaporation.

New Research

Scientists are helping in several ways. They do research to find better farm chemicals which do less harm than ones used now. They also breed new varieties of crops which are resistant to the diseases and pests. Crops which do not need so much fertilizer to make them grow could also be developed.

Closed Tunnels

A whole variety of crops will be grown in closed plastic tunnels, keeping in the nutrients and water. This prevents the water being wasted by evaporation and protects soils from becoming too salty.

Salty Soil

In Western Australia, new crop trees, such as pistachio, carob, oak and tree lucerne, are being planted to draw down the water in the soils. They will also help to produce shade and prevent the soil from becoming salty.

Transporting Food

Growing the right crops in the right place is very important. It is not wise to try to grow tropical crops in heated greenhouses in a cold country. But transporting tropical crops to cold countries uses a lot of energy as well.

The way we transport food will change. Old canals and waterways can be re-opened and put into working order. Barges could carry large amounts of food. Fleets of super cargo ships, carrying vast amounts of goods, will be driven partly by the wind. They will have special metal sails which are controlled by computers and will turn to catch the wind.

Even giant airships may help to transport our food around the world.

During the years of good harvests, surplus food may even be stored away for the future in containers deep in the ocean. There the temperature is always a cool 38°F (4°C). Food will stay fresh for a long time if it is kept away from oxygen in an atmosphere of nitrogen.

How You Can Help

If you have a large enough backyard, it is perfectly possible for you to grow enough fruit and vegetables, organically, to keep your family going.

With a bit of help, you might even keep chickens for their eggs and a cow or goat for milk.

It could be great fun but it would be hard work. And you would have to get used to marks on the fruit and vegetables, and a few maggots inside. But there are no real worries. If anything went badly wrong, you wouldn't starve. You could just pop down to the local store or supermarket. People in poor countries aren't so lucky.

We can all help by making sure we eat a healthy, well-balanced diet, not too little and certainly not too much.

Food from the Sea

The sea provides us with food and it feeds all the different creatures living in it, from giant blue whales to tiny plankton, as well as millions of sea birds.

About 75 million tons of fish are taken out of the sea every year. They are sold as fresh fish, filleted and frozen, and dried and salted. Fish are an important food that contain vitamins, minerals and oils. They are also turned into animal feeds and fertilizers.

Saving the Stocks

In many places, the fleets of fishing boats are catching too many fish. They use modern technology to find the shoals and they scoop up everything in their path. If they catch too many fish or all the small, young ones, the fish cannot breed fast enough to replace themselves. Because of this the world's stock of fish is in grave danger.

Useful Seaweed

For thousands of years, farmers have used seaweed as organic fertilizers for their fields. Much of the waste from fish farms could be mixed with seaweed and composted, ready to be returned to the land.

Scientists study how many fish there are in one area of the sea and decide on how much can be caught without damaging the stocks. They then give quotas, or amounts, to each country's fishing fleets. The problem is how to control all the international fleets and make sure they do not catch more fish than they should.

During World War II, it was very dangerous to fish in the North Sea and the northeast Atlantic. Very few fish were caught, so they were given a long rest and their numbers increased.

Starving Birds

Catching too many sand eels in the North Sea is one reason why tens of thousands of sea bird chicks have starved to death on the Shetland Islands, off the coast of Scotland.

Saving the Whales

Thanks to the efforts of many thousands of people, most nations of the world have agreed to stop hunting whales and dolphins. We must all work very hard to make sure that they never change their minds and start killing again.

The world's nations must also pass laws to stop the overfishing of the food which whales and dolphins eat.

Sport Fishing

One of the most popular outdoor sports is fishing. People pay immense amounts of money for fishing tackle and the right to fish in rivers, lakes and reservoirs.

In the past, protests from fisherman have forced many industries and sewage works to clean up their processes and stop polluting these waters.

Some people argue that fishing is a cruel sport and is senseless, especially when the fish are not eaten. This is one of those ethical questions. What do you think?

Trout Farms

Freshwater trout farms show great promise. The fish are raised in special tanks and fed on waste from other parts of the food industry. But all large farms of any sort produce waste which pollutes the local rivers.

Farming the Seas

Fish farms certainly seem to be one answer to the demand for more fish. They could take pressure off the sea fish stocks.

Oyster and mussel farms were the first real success stories, and cause the least problems. This is because they feed by filtering the natural crop of plankton from the water. A spin-off from the oyster farms is the cultivation of pearls.

Salmon and other fish farms have been set up off the coasts in many countries. The fish are bred in large cages floating on the water. As waves can smash the strongest things, the cages are put in the most sheltered places. But waste from the fish and the chemicals which keep the fish free from parasites and diseases pollute the water. Chemicals which stop seaweed growing on the cages may poison other life in the sea.

It may be possible to move the cages slowly along to spread the waste. Experiments are also being made with cages which are built in the open sea where the currents would carry away the waste. During storms, these can be lowered down to calm water below the waves.

Shrimp and crab farms are now a great success in tropical countries. They are kept in tanks on land, with seawater pumped in. But they must be fed and that food must come from somewhere. The waste they produce must also be dealt with.

Seaweed farming is also a success. More people are able to enjoy the delights of Far Eastern cooking which makes delicious use of seaweed.

The Human Race

Every second of every hour of every day, three babies are born. They are extra members of the crew of Spaceship Earth. Like you, they need enough food, clothes, a warm bed and lots of clean water to drink and to be washed in. They need a doctor to look after them, and a secure future.

Most parents hope that their children will do well at school and get good jobs when they graduate. They also hope that, one day, their children will have children of their own. The world is faced with the problem of a rapidly growing population. This is a problem that will not solve itself.

Unequal Shares

Sadly, fewer and fewer of the new crew members have much hope of enough food, water, homes and a future. This is because most of them live in the poor Third World. The resources of our Spaceship Earth are shared out very unequally.

Draw a line across the map of the world just north of the Equator. Most of the rich nations of the world live above this line. The 25% of the crew who live above the line use 80% of all the wealth, goods and resources of Spaceship Earth. The other 75% of the crew have to make do with the 20% that is left.

Large Families

Then why, you may ask, do the parents in the poor countries go on having huge families when parents in the richer countries have only two or three children?

The answer is that in the rich countries, most people are educated and they understand how to limit their families. Most parents also realize that it is better to have fewer children. Then they can afford all the things which go with modern life – a comfortable home with everything they need, a car and vacations.

They also know that, thanks to pensions and social security, they will be looked after in their old age.

In the poor countries, the opposite is true. More children mean more hands to work on the farm or to beg for food. And the parents have a better chance, or the only chance, of being looked after when they are old and cannot work.

Exploding Population

In the rich countries, there are now lots of old people. This is because people live longer, thanks to good food and medical care. There are lots of grandfathers and grandmothers who have stopped having babies, and fewer young people who will have children in the future.

In the poor countries, it is quite different. There, most people do not live to an old age because of the lack of food and medicines. The vast majority of people, in some countries more than 60%, are young and have not started to have children yet.

Even if these young people were persuaded to limit their families to two children, the population would continue to explode for the next 25 years at least.

Now, if you are tempted to say: "Why should we worry? We have got our population growth in order, it's their problem," please stop and think.

When you are starving, own no land, no possessions except a few old cans and bottles, there is nothing you can give up to solve the problems. Remember, most of the poor people who have nothing would like to be like us, who have all we need.

We, in the rich part of the world, have so much. We each use up 30 – 40% more of the world's resources than the poor countries. So we are part of the problem. What is more, we can afford to do something about it.

We must now set a good example in all things for the future.

The human race is now on. It is a race for survival and we must all play our part.

Organizations You Can Join

There are many organizations that are working to help Spaceship Earth. You, your friends and your parents can join one or more of them. Some of them have special junior sections and local branches. You can write to them for information and membership.

Adopt-an-Acre Program
The Nature Conservancy
1815 N. Lynn Street
Arlington, VA 22209
Adopt a piece of the rainforest.

America Oceans Campaign
725 Arizona Avenue
Suite 102
Santa Monica, CA 90401
Provides information about our oceans.

Center for Marine Conservation
1725 DeSales Street, NW
Suite 500
Washington, D.C. 20036
This organization protects marine habitats.

Defenders of Wildlife
1244 19th Street, NW
Washington, D.C. 20036
Interested in endangered species and wildlife legislation.

Global ReLeaf
P.O. Box 2000
Washington, D.C. 20013
An organization working to save forests.

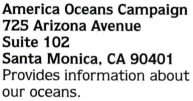

American Rivers Conservation Council
322 Fourth Street, NE
Washington, D.C. 2006
Dedicated to preserving America's scenic rivers.

The Children's Rainforest
P.O. Box 936
Lewiston, Maine 04240
Through this group, children can buy and preserve parts of the Costa Rican rainforest.

The Greenhouse Crisis Foundation
1130 17th Street, NW
Washington, D.C. 20036
Provides current information on global warming.

Kids for a Clean Environment
P.O. Box 158254
Nashville, TN 37215
An environmental organization for kids.

Woodsy Owl Campaign
U.S. Department of Agriculture
Forest Service,
P.O. Box 96090
Washington, D.C. 20090-6090
This group works to increase children's awareness of the environment. Provides free materials such as coloring sheets and stickers.

Sierra Club
730 Polk Street
San Francisco, CA 94109
Promotes responsible use of the Earth's ecosystems and resources.

National Audubon Society
950 Third Avenue
New York, NY 10022
Dedicated to conservation.

Smokey Bear and Fire Prevention
Smokey Bear Headquarters
U.S. Forest Service
1621 North Kent Street
Room 1001 RPE
Rosslyn, VA 22209
Makes available posters, comic books, and bookmarks to make children aware of the campaign to fight fires.

World Wildlife Fund
1250 24th Street, NW
Washington, D.C. 20037
The WWF works internationally to protect endangered lands and wildlife.

To locate your nearest Recycling Center:
Dial 1-800-CALL-EDF
(Environmental Defense Fund)

Nature Conservancy
1800 North Kent Street
Suite 800
Arlington, VA 22209
Seeks to preserve ecological diversity through protection of natural areas.

Index